HIS OWN INVENTED TORMENTS
THOMAS SHARP

First printing 2021

All rights reserved. No part of this publication may be reproduced, stored in a retrieval system or transmitted in any form or by any means, electronic, mechanical, photocopying, recording or otherwise, without prior permission in writing from Thomas Sharp.

The moral rights of the author have been asserted.
www.thepoetryofitall.com
Instagram @thomassharp

The mysteries of existence are complex, entangled, obscure, vague, esoteric, ungraspable and maddening. My poetry isn't trying to solve any of it. The only answer is that there is no answer.

I'm interested in poetry as an attempt to sculpt language into infinite rooms for readers to step into. A virtual reality to play in.

Magic, by which I mean the occult, is a technology for bending reality through altered consciousness. Poetry can be a temporal consciousness experience. What will then happen is up to you.

Stepping into poems can be made easier with keys. David Lynch famously included ten 'clues' to understanding *Mulholland Drive* as an insert in the DVD release. I don't offer clues, there's nothing to work out here, but I do offer concepts that were important to me in writing *His Own Invented Torments*.

1. John Milton's *Paradise Lost*, a long poem about the fall of Lucifer and then of humankind, is like a Sun Ra and his Arkestra psychedelic cosmic jazz album. It's a throbbing swirl of colour. The broken rainbow on the cover of this book is my riff on a Gustave Doré illustration.

2. I began a mythopoeia in *myu*, a long poem about one second in the consciousness of the universe in 1913, written through Active Imagination. *The Sacrifice* and *The Tree* are both extracts from *myu*.

3. '*In the beginning was the Word*' we are told, and so a skit on language follows myu creating everything.

4. Our contemporary fall is the climate crisis. *Totems* is a vision of a solarpunk, regenerative future. The language is an imagining of how a post ecological-disaster culture might speak. Their horror words relate to climate change, '*floodolence*', '*gaiashakes*', '*bergmelt*', '*hurricursed*'. They don't use the word '*the*' to refer to other aspects of nature, if they did it would imply a remove, which led to the disaster. So '*us*' replaces '*the*'.

5. *Sacrifice* is a kiss to Rupert Brooke. *Azazel* (Satan's standard bearer), is the same poem set years later. Young men dying in war – both the privileged and the masses. Climate change may be even more egalitarian in its cruelty.

6. The final poem – a reversal of a usual structure in which an everyday detail is mused upon to draw a wider meaning – is related to *Totems* and ties back to the opener.

Poems

What will
How to invent a magic trick
Rue the dire event
Giant Tube Worms
The Tree
Abstract Thoughtlines ...
New Ecstatic Songs of Gnosis
The Sacrifice
Azazel
The ancients were making it up too
Evie
The nearest Bishop
The Wrong Romantic
Blue
I button my shirt
If I have ever been loved
Supernovas and blueberry donuts
5am on the shore of Lake Coniston

What will
it would've
taken myu
to make the all.
(Scholars will say
myu is the all
and that is that,
but that is why
they are flattened
scholars, not children
balancing stones.)
Children know
myu Was
and then, in an act
of cascading aeonloud
laughter and will,
began the precarious
things.
Writing a poem
is balancing stones.
Beginning everything
is what happens
when reading one.
What will.

How to invent a magic trick

Magicians, by which I mean
conjurors, are the glamour margin
of the logician field. They imagine
a reaction, a yielding of reality
in the supine mind of one resigned
to the quotidian, and then design
backwards. In action, a welding of stages,
each judicious, pragmatic, sagacious,
each almost preterite, no shenanigans,
no wielding of power, until, remarkably,
the prestige alights, by which I mean,
the imperious impossible that slackens
the quotidian in an instant. Did I say
magician? I lack words. I meant politician.

Rue the dire event

In my cell of grey shame,
chained within 'if only's,
where dreaming is Houdiniing,
I nostalgise your eyes.

Adoring them was obvious
for all of us. I'd fallen for
their milky gold,
their whale-calf blue,
the startle of each day.

Once helium silver,
then a ready-tongue pink
troping, trading into
every sunset ever seen.

Rainbow banquet of gaze.
Wavelengths of rarity.
A nettle-sting sparkling
in eyes of invisible ink.

Hues from a star's deepest chamber,
brightness pressed on itself,
painting everything in
an awefull desert glare.

In the hour of the flood,
I'd heard,
your orbs were terrible waters,
drowning purple, shattered wood,
woemen and children gulping
all the way down.
You were so cruel,
oh, to be heat by your side
and then see receding change
in eyes of bluebell, church lilac
and lily wonce more.

I will scorch everything
to be coloured
by your looke again.

Giant Tube Worms

When the saidnow news of smothering ecological
apocalypse had been assimilated into the culture,
we all could relax once more. It hadn't been the heat —
'Martin, order more refrigerators' — that was stressful
it was the exhaust headache of dystopian art everywhere,
frankly we could do with some love songs again.
And just in time, away from the fattening of the water,
a group of young thems started being fucking vital
in plume-like vascularised clothes. Undersea
rift worms vampiring on the energy of a volcanic vent.
We'd not realised, living far too close to ourselves,
that evolution had always been a hot and sexy circle.

The Tree

The tree is an enthusiasm of pulsing chlorophyll,
branches creaking like gossiping harbour boats,
it hosts a begatting of greens –
the eye-green of a deepriver fish trancing the reed roots
thinking forgotten-mud slow,
begats the spritegreen of atmospheric electrical phenomenon
only the black satellite can see
begats gangrene-green,
chop-it-off green,
bite-leather-and-think-of-the-Lickey-Hills green,
begats witches' milk green,
begats the spiky and dark-sermon green of a Christmas wreath.
The tree moves as one thousand unfaithful mouths.
The tree smells like the earthworms' god,
of ever-shifting shade, of wooded acceptance.
It has a scent so wise and nuanced,
so placidly fungal, so soul slow,
it feels like awareness was always this.
The tree moves like a new mother.

Abstract Thoughtlines Written In Front Of Totem 23h9 Long After The Tip

Our totems are totems to nothing
before they stand hang dissect us sky
before a mind a million meanings full.

Structural ambiguity is of primacy
in their printing and plan. The minor
intelligences downtime-design them

(between determining

flight-path corrections and routine-surgery)
avoiding animalistic and anthropomorphic forms.
(And we cured ourselves of pareidolia

five seasons ago with a complex protein fold,
(ironically us genetic technician
who ran the programme saw the pattern,

marvelling 'a frowning face I perceive'),
it had to be done we'd begun to love
delivery automata like children

even through the Feature Laws prohibited
human-like appearances, the businesses
still released appliance arrangements that prayed

upon an infant in us longing for mother).
Our totems are totems to nothing.
Psychological prompts. Identity psychopomps.

Seasonmiddle so us daysky variates
a ripe citrus swatch effected by
an everever of elleedee particle-drones
colouring The Great Heavy.

(Abundant birds unseen opened throats)

Pleasurable senseload,
calming, stimulating,
resembles being a jellyfish
thinking through us
fluorescent present.

(Territorial melodies abandoned to everyheaven)

Matching a barchart of a relatively stable system,
a mauve ridge of squared mountains
x-axis an indistinct distance.

(Bergmelt beauty of all us avian code)

From the solar fields topping each,
unsignalling glints of balking, bouncing sun.
Photons caulking us darkstuck nearside plane.

(Mating music spilling brightshine pollocky)

Around me us trees,
megahanced by chlorophyll steroids,
thrive under limed air.

I hear them growing
and they sound like fire advancing,
though tiny and slowed.

'What are you seeing'
I say to my friend
leaving no question mark
at sentence end.

Psychological prompts. Identity psychopomps.

'I see respectful vines
ozymandering a braincarved torso'
they reply, a trace of unworked
issue in their neutralvocal.

'Maybe a relic, certified-remain,
unregenerative art, uglythoughted
in its floodolence of deciding.
It's narrow-band-black-white certain.'

To be certain is to be
hurricursed we are taught.
The Pastors before The Tip
were certain of everything.

Us home blooms today with
an unfocus of fauvist petals
programmed to approximate
applause as colour.

Flowers strengthen towers
we are taught, a composite
that offers aesthetics and
proof against us gaiashakes.

I derivé us biggerhome,
first through fast fields
of repair temples and exchanges,
then through slow fields
of places of silence solitary.

I buy a paper book of poetry
from the time of the Pastors,
distasteful and of interest.
Sitting in a garden dialed
to high mutate, a lute player
in the corner mimicking a heart,
I read a poem and smile –
they were so pleased with progress.

New Ecstatic Songs of Gnosis

A siliconKing propulses dumbrockets,
like dandelion clocks,
into the face of space to crumbburst
with satellitic merriment. One pre-history night,
cloudless and dinosaurcold,
we climb the roof, swing from ancient aerials
and amaze at a riversnake of new stars
processing mathematically mythic.
We are thankful
someone has finally tidied the heavens.

Mysteryteams of institutionalised prophets
tend the big belly.
They scatter particlepackets into the fast,
then listen for voices from ventriloquists.
One stonesteady morning, eggs on bubble
like amoeba, bacon spinning in its hiss,
we read of the new physics,
the new folds and curves we now live in,
and we are thankful
someone has finally defined the spirits' tug.

Patternanaesthetised programmers
in Jacquard Loom warpweftwarp
and job-locked rows + columns,
work in the warm HUM of extrapolation.
One hunting evening, circling sex,
citywet, we slip like spears
into a gallery called *The Cave*
to wounder at an installation of AIart.
We are thankful
someone has finally controlled the symbols.

The Sacrifice

Look! The youngrich are rapture bright,
with skin that soaks up all the light.
All the light that touches them
remains as gem or anadem.
Steady glow, empire-stable,
morning-caught at breakfast table.
Deeper though, through constant dapple
in the tiny family chapel,
under the Burne-Jones window scenes
which winter-shine with John's dark dreams,
the light from these a nurse's milk,
nourish of colour, tender silk.
The world sea, horse-blue in its lashings,
the Babylon-red of beastly thrashings.
The richyoung keep their caresses,
stardew gilds their eased successes.
Buttercup spots on beach-brown tummy
from drunkenly adoring mummy.
Indian veranda blaze,
candlelit bops in Oxbridge days.

They keep it all, absorbed and worn –
bring every dawn to those high-born!
To those comfortable in their vowels,
who fuck in bluebells, fuck with howls
at the radiance of being,
at light's selective seeing.
They take it in. They take it all.
Delicate and untouchable.
Prometheus's gift unspun,
they sing the anthem of sun.
And soon, some, in the field's fast flare
and mugwhump blast will brighten there.
Brighter and brighter and brighter
they'll get, brighter and brighter.

And is there the blinding ecstasy
of mummy's true God still for tea?

Azazel

I'm sweating words in a desert
dry as a staked goat's yell.
Sweating swear words in the exhale
of a bomb, roadside, homemade.

I miss my mom. Spectral memory
of her nervy blue smoking,
tapping a dull-gold foil carton on
our *Sharkskin Grey* plastic dashboard

as I cheerio'd the car
to sign up at Sankeys Corner.
The wind on the high street
was a camouflage for sorrow.

I'd never been further than
Birmingham before. Now
standard bearer for the family,
hero of the snooker club,

mentioned between explosive red breaks,
automatic blue chalk action,
quick disappears of pink,
and quick disappears of light

Angel Lager halves in the penumbra
of each blazing table. I remember
a brown-sauce bacon sandwich
on a hangover back-garden lawn

one New Year's Day, grass tarted
up with frost, little glam rockers.
A blackbird pop song blasting
from Mrs Stannard's chip-yellow fence.

Inside, my sister, who loved Christmas,
was in heaven with her new make-up.
Outside, my dad, never well, had a face
the colour of Villa's claret scarves.

The ancients were making it up too

Light thin tea-tray, red
as the dye added
to the plastic, pop it
on the formica with a click.

Twenty-three tea-lights lit,
arranged free of pattern,
seemingly, then the tray is handed
solemn tenderly to Mom.

A May Day fire-leap to brightmeet
Belenus with longleg and shout,
a-whacking of the fly-escorted
heavy flank of summer to urge it in.

But Dad is but but whatif
bonfirenervous – furious neighbours
are death. Scorched earth
a blight on best-keptness,

a breadth of Gaia rubbed out
forever, a patch of particle-black
ruin running carbon rivers
in the bungalow rains.

So clever Mom lays down
a host of candles, neat solution,
like a religious system,
an improvised tea-tray pantheon ...

a-tisket-a-tasket and spring over!
Three times a fair number!
Rattling pecking-cheers from their livers,
arms out like sewing-basket ribbons!

Suburban hedges growl.
Days circle in green.
The slow pounce
of lawn growth begins.

Light thin tea-tray, red
as the dye added
to the plastic, pop it
on the formica with a click.

Evie

Thinning darkness,
before cigarettes and news,
when men who must be jovial
move the rose-ing dawn
on chorus-squeaking castors,
to form modest market stalls.

She enters invented streets,
an unfulfilled snake of a string bag
coiling cardiganed bone.

Greeted by name,
'Evie, my love',
but still a pantomime
of fruit-squeezing frowns –
she'll not be seduced again.

Vegetables language
in remembered shades –
of lorry bruisings,
whitening waves of lettuce,
potatoes polished pale by sack.

The carrots are old politicians,
harping on glory days of purple.
Leeks have let their green slip away.

Bananas in yellowgangs.
Peaches in smug.
Apples ripen to see her.
Rapturous reddlement.

Colour enough for another fallen day.

The nearest Bishop

with appleeys
fruit-fly rapid,
has the fiery
sleep
of flooded rivers.

Smothersnow,
brides-a-birthing,
sailors returning
say
innocence is white.

Shame? Graves-at-dusk
blue, a hidden death,
intangible
shadows of old life.

Blame reflected,
he walked on in
false bright hue,
a white-flame beyond blue,
forging
Adamantine chains.

The Wrong Romantic

A storm!! The following morning
(the model for all vampires)
locals living a whole life lakeside
(the model for all vampires)
said 'once in a decade'
with a mountain's frenzied awe.

I confess (the model for all vampires)
that as ordinary weather festered electric
I pulled out my collected Byron
(the model for all vampires)
for some grand poetic gothic posturing.

Lightning in cheap, paperback paper sheets
(I am so lonely) flips the water
and old man mountain glares sudden,
day-furious at 1am, over
the angled house on the vast shore
with its roof of black wing
and a turret for pinching the view.

Storm!! In unbelievable night
the hills lord on the far
in rapid static pathetic
of overwhelming entitled light
(the model for all vampires).

'Once in a decade' should
be unnecessary — the show
was violent and impressive enough —
but they made it feel special
(the model for all vampyres)
as did reading him.

And Polidori, doomed at falling flashing
birth, we couldn't save you,
physician chronicler of the other
Prometheus, and I am sorry
but not everyone is saved.

Blue

My rightnow sky
is ultra-calmexcitement blue.
It holds an overwhelming nothing
and is bigger than my heart.

It is a pupil to look through,
a master painter's single, sutured brushing,
the opposite of cherry blossom,
a perfect love affair, a mirror
reflecting just one perfect high.
It is bigger than my heart.

I keep choosing tarot cards
that futuresay I must let go.
Falling upwards is terribly hard
you know, fooling uncontrollably up
into ultra-calmexcitement blue.

I button my shirt

Carefulling from night's hold,
the freshlit morning considers winter.
Of what's coming a tiny low mist
whispers to the lawn. The air is magic
in its cold, quiet. The flowers are quiet and cold.

I button my shirt at the country hotel window,
look down on a lover, risen before everyone,
exploring the garden explaining it to herself.

She's shying through an overhung path.
A soaked branch slight unhooks from another,
swings with dew-bombed cavalier leaves
straight into her face. My lover.

A crackle of crows sudden UFO
from the see-far oak, clattering
open the day. Resolving to say
nothing at breakfast, I button my shirt.

If I have ever been loved

If I have ever been loved,
may it be for what I love in myself.
And if I have never been loved
little boy, it'll be because
I could not accept myself. Acceptance
metaphor. The morning bomber's mothering hum.
Lulled, August-white sky.
Even coldmountain echoes
pacify, like milk.
Nuclear codes radio in.
Belly doors open with a rich man's pride.
An atomic cloud sucks up itself selfishly
and sucks up all the shadows of the city
into the impossible entelechial object.
Generals and pilots accept that this is what
they must do and you, too, must accept that
this is what the unloved do.
If I have ever been loved,
may it be for what I love in myself.

Supernovas and blueberry donuts

We live between
supernovas and blueberry donuts.
Aeonic imagination, immediate sensation.

How beautiful is the insistent velvet
of a horse's nosing trust? And afternoons
when rain terribles the sky, leaving no place
for light? And afterwards, when light noses back
and trees shake a toughearth scent over everyone,
how beautiful is it all?

When I am a star I'll take my time to explode.
I'll bloom in the black crackle of space,
exploring all the wavelengths.
Until then, give me sugar.

5am on the shore of Lake Coniston

Here the world is ... now, there's a
self-centred start, this isn't the world,
everywhere are other centres, where
others are burning through their lives.

Here the early morning is ... again, no,
to be time-locked is to be the lake,
shimmering-ignorant of the sea, thinking
swells are the troubling of eternity.

Well then, let's begin with
the things I am aware of ...
ah, but see that division between me
and the all – that way war lies –

maybe ... what my awareness is
endlessly brushing ... closer, though
still a lapsarian disconnect, instead, perhaps,
what my consciousness joins ...

yes!, that's it! so we open ...
here what my consciousness joins ...
is vigorous in its stillness.

New sunlight an electrolyte etching on the water
of what ripples look like to the artist.
Fresh birdsong its mirror – acoustic etching on air.

A brief fish turmoil in the lake on my left,
behind me a fenced field swung into shadow
by deep trees which gathered years ago.

A dozy meadow still damp from night's dark foam,
though on the dawn-burning edges
dew is returning to the sky.

Sheep in the field have idled nearer,
thoughtless, solid, rough, snagable,
feet full of secret skips,
their business the steady tearing of grass.

Other works by Thomas Sharp

English Pan
The Sun Behind The Sun
Twelve Moons of Madness
All The Hauntings
The Mysteries
Naomi's Poem
Twenty-five sculptures in five dimensions
The Weeping Cufflinks
The longmonth of rumours of lights
myu
Selected Workings 2017-2020
Jack and Jill
Game Six

www.thepoetryofitall.com